JACKIE
KENNEDY ONASSIS

WOMAN OF COURAGE

KENNEDY ONASSIS

Catherine Corley Anderson

Lerner Publications Company ■ Minneapolis

ACKNOWLEDGMENTS

Archive Photos, 22, 37, 75, 78, 80; Bettmann Archive, 15; © Phil Burchman, 27; John F. Kennedy Library, 6, 34, 42, 51, 54, 55, 56, 58, 60, 66, 68, back cover; © Robert Meservey / © Molly Thayer Collection / Magnum Photos; Reuters / Bettmann, 2, 84, 86, 87 (both); © 1995 Jacques Lowe, front cover; UPI / Bettmann, 1, 8, 9, 12, 21, 24, 26, 28, 30, 33, 39, 43, 44, 49, 53, 57, 59, 64, 67, 69, 70, 71, 72, 74, 77, 81, 88 (both); UPI / Bettmann Newsphotos, 11, 50, 82.

This book is available in two bindings:
Library binding by Lerner Publications Company
Soft cover by First Avenue Editions
241 First Avenue North
Minneapolis, MN 55041

LIBRARY OF CONGRESS CATALOGING-IN-PUBLICATION DATA

Anderson, Catherine Corley
    Jacqueline Kennedy Onassis : woman of courage / by
Catherine Corley Anderson.
        p.   cm. — (Achievers)
    ISBN 0-8225-2885-1 (lib. bdg.)
    ISBN 0-8225-9714-4 (pbk.)
    1. Onassis, Jacqueline Kennedy, 1929–1994 — Juvenile
literature. 2. Celebrities—United States—Biography—Juvenile
literature. 3. Presidents' spouses—United States—Biography—
Juvenile literature. 4. Kennedy, John F. (John Fitzgerald),
1917–1963—Juvenile literature. I. Title. II. Series
CT275.0552A66   1995
973.922′092—dc20   94-37241
[B]   CIP
                                                                 AC

Manufactured in the United States of America
1   2   3   4   5   6   –   JR   –   00   99   98   97   96   95

Contents

Jackie Bouvier at age four on Long Island, New York

1

Young Days

Young Jacqueline Lee Bouvier had her mother's beautiful brown eyes and wavy, thick brown hair. Her face was shaped more like her father's—square-jawed, straight-nosed—and she had his straight, dark eyebrows. On little Jacqueline, the combination was very pleasing.

Jacqueline was born on July 28, 1929, in Southampton, New York. Jackie always felt closer to her father than to her mother, Janet Lee Bouvier. Janet was a cool, proper society matron and a noted horsewoman. As a mother, she was rather strict and was not above spanking her daughters if she felt they needed it.

Jackie competed at the sixth annual horse show of the Southampton Riding and Hunt Club in 1934. She is shown here with her parents, Janet and Jack Bouvier.

Jackie's father, Jack Bouvier (often called "Black Jack" because of his suntanned skin, dark blue eyes, and glistening black hair) was easygoing and indulgent with his daughter. The two of them spent wonderful days together, taking trips to the zoo, the ice cream parlor, toy stores, and dress shops. When her mother came along, they often went to horse shows, where Jackie was dressed in a tiny replica of her mother's riding outfit—top hat, ascot tie, coat with contrasting collar, trousers to match, and long leather boots.

Young Jackie was a self-possessed little girl. Her mother taught her to ride a horse when she was very young. Janet told her daughter, "Never fall off a horse, but if you do, get up and get right back on again." Perhaps this philosophy had something to do with the determination that Jackie showed later in her life.

Jackie often went riding with her mother. They are shown here in 1935.

When Jacqueline was five, she took part in the annual East Hampton Village Fair dog show. She showed her Great Dane, named King Phar. A newspaper wrote about the event, commenting that "Miss Jacqueline Bouvier showed her dog, which was about the same size as she."

Although the family appeared to be wealthy, Black Jack had made several bad investments and was deeply in debt. He was a stockbroker, but he had never been much of a businessman. He was much more interested in perfecting his suntan, buying expensive clothes, and spending money on his various lady friends.

As more and more of Black Jack's ventures failed, he began to drink heavily. He came from a wealthy family, and his wife's family, the Lees, were also wealthy. James Lee, Janet's father, loaned Jack money and provided the family with a rent-free, 11-room apartment on Park Avenue. There didn't seem to be much chance of Jack ever being able to repay his debts. In fact, Janet and Black Jack spent even more borrowed money on lavish decorations for the apartment, two maids, a cook, a summer home on Long Island, and vacations. Neither Jack nor Janet knew how to live within their means.

When Jackie was three and a half, a baby sister, Caroline Lee, was born. Everyone called her Lee.

Their English nanny, Bertha Newey, took the girls to Central Park every day when the weather was nice. One day Jackie wandered away from her nanny and little Lee. She saw a policeman and walked up to him. The policeman looked down and said, "Are you lost, little girl?"

Jackie shook her dark curls. "No sir," she said, "but my nurse and baby sister are."

Jackie with her baby sister, Lee, in Central Park

Her worried mother found her at the police station, after the distraught nurse had hurried home to tell her Jackie was missing. Jackie was perfectly at ease with the police officers, no doubt telling them about her pony or her handmade doll, Sammy, with whom she had long, imaginary conversations.

Jackie holds her doll, Sammy, as she poses with her mother in East Hampton, Long Island.

Jackie and Lee, unaware of the family's financial difficulties, enjoyed riding the elevator in the apartment building where they lived. One day they scurried in, and Lee looked up at the elevator operator, who had a shock of blond hair standing straight up from his forehead.

"You look pretty today, Walter (or whatever his name was)," she said.

Jacqueline turned to her sister and scolded, "That's not true, Lee; you know very well he looks like a chicken."

Jackie's parents had not been close for a long time. Money and women were at the core of the problem—Jack's continual failures on the stock market and his extramarital affairs. Finally, Janet divorced him. She was given custody of the children during the week, and Jack had them on alternate weekends and during half of Christmas, Easter, and summer vacations. In reality, however, a tug-of-war between the two parents began, each vying for the affection of their young daughters.

Jackie, almost 11, was crushed by the divorce of her parents. She adored her handsome, dashing father. In her eyes, he could do no wrong. Her personality began to change. Instead of the outgoing child she had been, she became quiet and withdrawn. She wandered about, lonely and confused. Her father took a small, four-room apartment in New York. Janet and the two girls moved to a smaller apartment at One Gracie Square.

According to the divorce agreement, Janet had to pay for all the girls' and her own clothes and their daily living expenses. Jack Bouvier agreed to pay his daughters' medical and dental bills and their school costs.

But Jack spent lavishly on his daughters, taking them to expensive restaurants, buying them clothes at shops that catered to the wealthy, and generally acting like money was no object. He was quite knowledgeable about women's styles, and he lectured them on what was good and bad in fashion.

Janet began to be seen with the wealthy and socially prominent Hugh D. Auchincloss. About four years after her divorce, she and "Hughie," as he was called, were married. Hugh owned a massive estate called Merrywood, in McLean, Virginia, and another beautiful home called Hammersmith Farm in Newport, Rhode Island.

Jackie's stepfather was kind, generous, and even-tempered. It was impossible not to like "Uncle Hughdie," as the girls decided to call him. Janet and Hugh divided their time between their two estates, and Jackie, Lee, and three children from Hugh's two previous marriages went with them. The number of times the girls stayed with their father was greatly reduced, and Jack Bouvier grew bitter. He was convinced that Janet conspired to turn his daughters completely away from him.

Jackie, now 13, was becoming a young woman. She was invited to many parties. Consciously or unconsciously, Jacqueline had developed a shy smile, a whispery, soft voice, and a manner that both attracted and puzzled many people. She was tall and slim, with a natural grace—a certain way of walking or entering a room with her head up and her back straight.

Ten-year-old Jackie with her dog Tammy

She attended Miss Porter's Finishing School in Farmington, Connecticut. There she received an excellent academic education and learned all the niceties of high society. She talked in a soft, well-modulated voice, never spoke out of turn, and always wore white kid gloves with formal clothes—some of the requirements of well-bred young women. When she graduated from Miss Porter's in June 1947, she was acknowledged by her teachers to be one of the outstanding students. She was especially gifted in history, literature, and art. One of the lessons she learned at Miss Porter's was the importance of rising to the occasion. When a woman was faced with a situation where something needed to be done, she did it herself, without running to someone else for help. It was a valuable lesson.

Jackie was also somewhat rebellious while at Miss Porter's. She rebelled against school rules and social mores. Once she even dumped a chocolate pie upside down in the lap of a teacher she especially disliked. When she graduated, her yearbook entry under "ambition in life" was "not to be a housewife."

One of the traditions for young women in high society was to have a "coming out" party—a formal introduction into the adult world. Society columnist Igor Cassini, who went by the name

"Cholly Knickerbocker" in his newspaper column, wrote about Jackie's coming out party, a formal dinner dance at the Clambake Club in Newport. He voted Jacqueline Bouvier "Debutante of the Year." A picture shows Jackie, almost 18, coming down a stairway, arms flung in the air in an abandonment of joy, her bouffant, white tulle overskirt floating behind her. She almost seemed to be flying. Her radiant smile proclaimed, "The world is my oyster." Would she open it up and find the pearl?

Jackie was named "Debutante of the Year" in 1947.

2

Coming of Age

After graduating from Farmington, Jackie spent two years at Vassar College, a women's college on the Hudson River in Poughkeepsie, New York. Jackie was an A student, but she was not especially interested in school activities outside of classes. While at school, she dated frequently but not any one person in particular. During July and August 1948, the summer of her freshman year, Jackie went to Europe with three friends and a chaperone. The group toured parts of England, France, Italy, and Switzerland. Jackie enjoyed the busy trip and vowed to return.

At the beginning of her sophomore year, she saw a notice on a school bulletin board describing a

Junior Year Abroad program at Smith College, a women's college in Northampton, Massachusetts. Without consulting either of her parents, Jacqueline applied to Smith for admission and was accepted. She wanted to attend classes at the Sorbonne, a famous university in Paris.

At first her parents both disapproved, but the reputation of the Sorbonne appealed to Janet's snobbishness. Black Jack was sure the whole idea was an Auchincloss plot to get Jackie away from him. When Jackie convinced him that she was going, however, he insisted on paying for the trip himself. He had promised to pay for her education and he did.

Jackie's junior year abroad began with two months in Grenoble, France, where she took an intensive French language course. She stayed with a French family and spoke only French. Then she moved to the Sorbonne in Paris, where she spent the rest of the school year. There, she chose to stay with another French family rather than live in Reid Hall, where most American students stayed. She studied French literature and history and reveled in the heady atmosphere of the Sorbonne. Compared to the hustle and bustle of Vassar, the French school was quiet and studious. Her year abroad also allowed Jackie some escape from the competition between her two parents for her attention.

In August 1949, Jackie, *center*, sailed to France to study at the Sorbonne, a famous university in Paris.

Jacqueline had a great sense of freedom in Paris. She went to the opera, theater, ballet, museums (especially the Louvre), jazz clubs, and cafés. Although she had many casual friends, she had difficulty feeling close to people and usually did not share her inner thoughts with others.

When she returned from France, Jackie decided to spend her senior year at George Washington University in Washington, D.C. Washington was a big city, and great things happened there. One of the people Jackie met in Washington was Charles Bartlett, Washington correspondent for the *Chattanooga Times*. On May 8, 1951, Charles and Martha Bartlett invited Jackie to a small dinner party at their home. Congressman John Kennedy was also a guest. Although they enjoyed each other's company, the idea that Kennedy was a politician did not impress Jackie. The couple did not see each other again until the following winter—again at one of the Bartletts' dinner parties.

During her senior year in college, Jackie attended George Washington University in Washington, D.C.

Jackie graduated from George Washington University in 1951. By then she spoke French, Italian, and Spanish fluently. Although still an amateur, she had also perfected her painting skill. She was becoming her own woman.

While attending GWU, Jackie had entered *Vogue* magazine's 16th annual Prix de Paris, a writing contest open to college seniors. The winner received a one-year trainee position with the magazine—six months in Paris and six months in New York. Jackie worked hard to meet the requirements of the contest, and her efforts paid off. Out of 1,280 entrants, Jackie won.

Uncle Hughdie, however, was not so happy about Jackie winning the contest. He did not want her to spend so much time in Paris, because he was afraid she would decide to stay there permanently. He talked her out of accepting the *Vogue* prize. Instead, he offered both Lee and Jackie a summer trip to Europe as a graduation present. Lee had graduated from Miss Porter's School. Eventually Jackie agreed. She and Lee traveled in England, France, Spain, and Italy, returning in late summer, 1951.

Much to the dismay of her mother, when Jackie returned from her European trip, she took a job with the Washington *Times-Herald* as its Inquiring Reporter. She had to approach complete strangers on the street, ask them a question, and request permission to take their picture. She seemed to be completely unsuited to the job, and it took all her courage. Her training at Farmington came to her aid—"rise to the occasion."

As an inquiring photographer for the Washington *Times-Herald,* Jackie is taking a picture of a woman feeding goldfish located in a rooftop pool.

Jackie did. As she became more experienced, her questions became witty and off-beat. Her column began to sparkle. Soon she was given more important assignments. Jackie began interviewing important people in the government and in society. By this time, Jack Kennedy was deeply involved in his first campaign for the Senate, and Jackie was engaged to John Husted, a young stockbroker in New York.

During this same period, Jack Kennedy spent the most of his time in Massachusetts, campaigning for the Senate. He sometimes saw Jackie during the middle of the week, when he was in Washington to attend to his duties as congressman. In March Jackie broke off her engagement. She commented that Husted was "immature and boring." However, when a friend asked what she thought of John Kennedy, her reply was, "Princeton and Harvard with rough edges." By April Jack and Jackie were dating more regularly. In November 1952, Jack won his Senate seat by the greatest majority ever in a Massachusetts election.

Eventually Jack Kennedy took Jackie to Hyannis Port, the Cape Cod town where the Kennedys still have a family compound—a private area with several houses. She met his mother and father as well as the rest of the family—a daunting experience. Jacqueline liked Jack's father, Joe Kennedy, at once. But Jackie and Rose Kennedy, Jack's mother, viewed each other a bit warily. The many brothers and sisters, girlfriends and boyfriends, in-laws, and children were a bewildering lot. Their seemingly endless energy, their teasing and joking and their rough games were somewhat overwhelming, but Jackie tried to take it all as a good sport. She loved the sailing, the swimming, and the long walks with Jack, but she never enjoyed the rough-and-tumble games of touch football—especially after a burly friend of Jack's ran into her, causing a broken ankle.

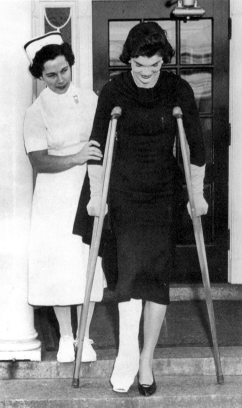

A nurse helps Jackie down some steps after she broke her ankle while playing touch football.

In the spring of 1953, the *Times-Herald* decided to send Jackie to London to cover the coronation of Elizabeth II on June 2. While she was gone, Jack wired her several times. One of the telegraphs read, "ARTICLES EXCELLENT, BUT YOU ARE MISSED." When Jack actually proposed marriage to Jackie is unclear. One account says that he proposed by telegraph while she was in London. Another states that he proposed just prior to her trip, and a third upon her return. In any case, they announced the engagement in the newspapers shortly after her return. They set their marriage date for September 12, 1953.

After the Senate election, Jack Kennedy saw Jackie frequently. Here, they are at Hyannis Port, Massachusetts.

Jacqueline Lee Bouvier and John Fitzgerald Kennedy were married in St. Mary's Catholic Church in Newport, Rhode Island. Joe Kennedy asked Archbishop Richard Cushing of Boston to conduct the ceremony. A reception in the spacious gardens of Hammersmith Farm followed. The wedding was the society event of the year.

Jackie looked beautiful wearing an ivory gown and her grandmother Lee's wedding veil. Jack was handsome in spite of a few scratches and bruises on his face—the result of a touch football game he played early on the morning of the wedding.

Jack and Jackie cut their wedding cake.

Bobby Kennedy, one of Jack's younger brothers, was best man, and Jackie's sister, Lee, was matron of honor. Jackie had wanted her father to give her away, and Jack Bouvier had been planning to do so. He had performed this duty for Lee and carried it off well. He checked into the Viking Hotel in Newport the day before the wedding, expecting to attend at least a few of the prenuptial parties. Unfortunately, however, he began drinking. When Janet learned about this, she refused to even let him attend the ceremony.

At the last minute, Hugh Auchincloss said he would give his stepdaughter away. The wedding was scheduled for noon. Jacqueline took the arm of her tall, impressive-looking stepfather, of whom she was very fond, and walked down the aisle with a smile. No one would know that there was a tiny ache in her heart for the father who wasn't there. It was the only flaw in an otherwise perfect day.

Jackie rode with Jack in a ticker tape parade in New York City during his 1960 presidential campaign.

3

Georgetown, Politics, Parties

After the wedding and the honeymoon in Acapulco, Mexico, Jack again plunged into his Senate duties. Jack and Jacqueline found a lovely estate in McLean, Virginia, not far from Washington or the Auchinclosses' Merrywood. Jackie set to work decorating their new home, keeping one part as a nursery. Both she and Jack wanted children, but her first pregnancy ended in a miscarriage.

Jack's bad back added to their problems. He had first injured it playing football in college and then injured it again during World War II, after which he underwent surgery in 1944. But he continued to be plagued by back pain. On October 11, 1954, Jack entered Cornell University Medical Center in

New York to undergo tests. His doctors wanted to find the cause of his chronic pain, and they decided he needed a spinal operation. Because he also had Addison's Disease, which lowers the body's resistance to infection, the operation posed a great risk. Just a little more than a year after their wedding, Jackie heard from the doctors that her husband had only a 50-50 chance of survival.

Jack wanted to have the operation in spite of the odds. It took place on October 21, with Jacqueline and all of the Kennedys praying for his recovery. An infection set in, however, and Jack went into a coma. Doctors notified Jackie and the rest of the family that Jack was near death.

Jackie and the Kennedy family stood at Jack's bedside as a priest gave him the last rites of the Catholic church. Surprisingly, after a few weeks Jack rallied and came out of the coma. By Christmas the hospital released him. He and Jackie spent the holidays at the Kennedy home in West Palm Beach, where he had to lie flat on his back. To add to the family's trauma, Jack's infection once again flared. Doctors told him that the operation would have to be repeated to remove a metal plate implanted during the first operation. Although the second operation, which took place in February, was successful, Jack was never without pain in his back.

Jack hobbled on crutches into Cornell University Medical Center for a spinal operation. Jackie carried his X-rays.

While flat on his back in the hospital, Jack decided to write a book. He called it *Profiles in Courage*, an account of eight senators who risked their careers in the cause of right and justice.

During her husband's illness, Jackie showed her courage and resilience. She spent every day with him. She brought in books and other materials that he needed for research. Ted Sorenson, Jack's legislative aide, also helped. Jackie took dictation and did the typing. When the book was published, it went immediately to the top of the best-seller list. Then it won the 1956 Pulitzer Prize for biography. Jack dedicated it "To my wife, Jacqueline, whose help during all the days of convalescence I cannot ever adequately acknowledge."

33

Jack autographs copies of *Profiles in Courage,* which he wrote—with Jackie's help—while flat on his back in the hospital.

In 1955 they acquired one of the houses at the Kennedy compound in Hyannis Port and made the final payment for Hickory Hill, their McLean home. Jackie became pregnant again early in 1956, expecting a child in September. In August she accompanied Jack to the Democratic National Convention in Chicago. Although Jack was nominated for vice president, he did not win the nomination. After the convention, Jack took a sailing vacation in southern France. Jackie decided to recuperate from the convention at Hammersmith Farm. On August 23, she suffered an internal hemorrhage and went into early labor. Doctors at Newport Hospital tried to save the baby, but the little girl was stillborn.

This was a difficult period in the Kennedy's marriage. Jack had not been there for Jackie when she most needed him. They both became withdrawn. Rumors of divorce began to circulate. Jackie was very unhappy and bitterly disappointed at failing to have a child for the second time. When Jack went off to campaign for presidential candidate Adlai Stevenson, Jackie went to New York to visit her sister, Lee. Jack once described Jackie's temperament by drawing a wavy line across a sheet of paper. Then he drew a bold, straight line through the first line to describe his own temperament. They both wondered if they were suited for each other.

Jackie often found it difficult to be part of the boisterous Kennedy clan. They were fiercely political. She had been taught to have a low opinion of most politicians. She also thought that politics conflicted with her own interests in art and literature. In an effort to solve some of these problems, she met with Joe Kennedy to see if some changes could be made. Joe agreed that when all the Kennedys and their families were gathered at Hyannis Port or West Palm Beach, they no longer had to eat dinner with Rose and Joe every night—

once a week would be enough. Jack agreed to stop taking phone calls during dinner. Although seemingly unimportant, these measures eased some of the strain.

She and Jack decided to sell the large McLean estate to Bobby and Ethel Kennedy, who were well on their way toward having a large family. From January until May 1957, Jack and Jackie rented a typical townhouse in Georgetown, an old but fashionable section of Washington, D.C. They gave some small dinner parties and attended a few cocktail parties. Jackie was a gracious hostess, and the food, the guests agreed, was very good.

In May the couple bought their own redbrick, Federal-style townhouse, built in 1812. Much to her delight, Jackie learned that she was pregnant again. This time she decided to avoid any activities that may have ended her earlier pregnancies. She tried to concentrate her efforts on decorating the new house at 3307 N Street NW. Jackie enjoyed fixing up the house to suit herself and Jack. She said she didn't want a house in which her husband would not be comfortable or in which children had to be told, "don't touch."

In early July, Jackie learned that her father was seriously ill. When she flew to New York to visit him, however, he seemed crabby but otherwise fine. He didn't know that he had cancer of the liver.

Jackie casts a critical eye on Jack's painting. She had given him the oil painting set for Christmas, 1953.

On August 3, Black Jack lapsed into a coma. This time both Jackie and Jack flew in to be with him, but he died an hour before they arrived. Jackie took charge of his funeral arrangements, feeling sad about his death and guilty for not being with him.

After the funeral, Jack and Jackie spent the rest of the summer in Hyannis Port, then returned to Washington and the new house. On November 27, 1957, the day after Thanksgiving, Jackie gave birth to Caroline Bouvier Kennedy at New York's Lying-In Hospital. Now at last, Jackie felt they were a real family. Their marriage improved, and they felt they couldn't have been happier.

Jackie reveled in being a mother. She once said, "If you don't do a good job of being a mother, nothing else you do well matters very much." Caroline had a British nanny named Maude Shaw to help take care of her, but Jackie saved a part of every day to spend with her little daughter. She got down on the floor to be on her level. She encouraged Caroline to take her first steps by holding out her teddy bear to entice her. Caroline made the important journey and fell triumphantly into her mother's waiting arms.

Jackie read to Caroline and made up stories to tell her. They played games together, sang songs, and chanted nursery rhymes. As Caroline got a little older, Jackie set up a little table with drawing and painting supplies next to her own easel. Mother and daughter painted happily together, although Jackie said Caroline just seemed to enjoy "making a mess" on her drawing paper.

At Hyannis Port, Caroline joined her Kennedy cousins in their busy comings and goings from one house to the other. They played hide-and-seek and follow-the-leader. If the games got too rough, Jackie took her daughter down to the beach. Caroline loved it when her mother swung her in a wide circle over the wild ocean waves. She called her father "Silly Daddy," and he called her "Buttons."

Jackie reads a story to Caroline at their summer home in Hyannis Port, Massachusetts. Jack also seems to be enjoying the tale.

When Jack ran for a second Senate term in 1958, Jackie thought she ought to help him with the campaign. She began appearing with him at meetings and campaign rallies. The old-line political experts thought Jackie was too refined, too pretty, and too fashionable. She would turn people off, they said. The opposite turned out to be true. Jackie's smile, her shyness, and her evident pride in her handsome and articulate husband was a boon to his campaign. Her ability to speak French, Spanish, and Italian was extremely helpful. When she spoke to a crowd in Boston's Italian-dominated North End in their own language, the people were thrilled. They felt Jackie was one of *them.* Jack won the election over a Republican Boston lawyer named Vincent Celeste by more than 874,000 votes—the largest majority ever achieved in Massachusetts.

Jackie stands next to Jack's photo as she speaks to voters during the Wisconsin primary campaign. Jack had to return to Washington for an important Senate vote on civil rights.

After his successful Senate race, Jack Kennedy, with the advice of others, decided to run for the Democratic nomination for the presidency. One of his chief Democratic rivals was Senator Hubert H. Humphrey of Minnesota. Because Jackie wanted to help in the effort, she accompanied him on campaign trips to New Hampshire, West Virginia, Wisconsin, California, Oregon, Ohio, Rhode Island, and New Jersey, during 1959 and half of 1960. Later she also went to Maine, Delaware, Tennessee, Kentucky, Maryland, North Carolina, New York, and Pennsylvania. Again she spoke to people in their native languages—Italian, French, and Spanish. In New York's Spanish Harlem, Jackie greeted a huge

40

crowd with *"Buenos días, mis amigos."* A thunderous cheer split the air. To those who criticized this tactic, Jackie said, "All of these people have contributed so much to our country's culture that it seems a proper courtesy to address them in their own tongue." Jackie also appeared on TV interview shows, visited supermarkets, and hosted luncheons.

In March 1960, while Jack and Jackie were campaigning for the Wisconsin primary election, an important civil rights vote came up in the Senate. Jack flew back to Washington to cast his vote, and Jackie carried on the campaign for him. She traveled from town to town giving short speeches. Most people expected Humphrey to win the Wisconsin primary because he lived in the neighboring state of Minnesota. But in the end, Jack won by 106,000 votes. Jackie's presence may have made the difference.

Kennedy entered and won primaries in seven states. His hard work paid off. In the 1960 Democratic National Convention in Los Angeles, Jack won the party's nomination on the first ballot. Now he would have to work even harder to win the November general election. His opponent, Richard M. Nixon, was well known because he had been vice president under President Dwight D. Eisenhower.

Jackie, *right rear,* and Jack, *center,* prepare for the television news show "Face the Nation."

In September 1960, Jackie began writing a newspaper column called "Campaign Wife," which helped bring her husband's views to the attention of female readers. She also kicked off the "Calling for Kennedy" week, a telephone campaign to get women's opinions on public issues.

Jackie was unlike previous campaign wives, and the American public was intrigued with her. She was refreshingly frank. She openly admitted that she rarely cooked and had little interest in housekeeping. She made it clear that she employed a governess for Caroline and had other household help as well. Some people thought she was too stiff and formal, but many others admired her character and demeanor. Jackie worked hard during the campaign, but she never enjoyed campaigning. She also missed Caroline.

During the 1960 presidential campaign, Jackie became pregnant again. As time went on, she had to curtail her traveling with Jack. She did join her husband in a ticker tape parade in New York not long before the election. She felt both exhilarated and fearful as their open car passed block after block of cheering, flag-waving crowds. Once their car was almost overturned by the press of thousands of enthusiastic supporters.

From then until election day, Jackie had only brief visits from her husband. Meanwhile, rumors about Jack's relationships with other women abounded.

During the 1960 presidential campaign, Jackie wrote a newspaper column called "Campaign Wife."

Jackie stands by his side as the new president-elect reads his acceptance speech the morning after the election.

4

A Long Night and a New Life

In Hyannis Port on the night of the election, everyone at the Kennedy compound except Jacqueline stayed up most of the night. Worn out by the excitement of the day and the soon-to-be-born baby, Jackie went to bed about 11:30.

Friends and family members gathered at Bobby and Ethel's house to await the results. The returns of the 1960 presidential election were the first to be tabulated by television computers. The reports about elections returns zigzagged. First Jack had a sizeable lead. Then Nixon was ahead. Then Jack pulled ahead again. At 3:00 A.M. Nixon appeared on TV. Everyone thought he would concede the election, but he didn't. Instead he said, "If the present trend continues..." Finally at 4:00 A.M., the Kennedy clan went to bed—still not knowing who had won.

When Jack awoke about 9:00 A.M., Caroline met her father with a big smile and said, "Good morning, Mister President." Jack laughed, lifted his daughter high in the air, then gave her a piggyback ride down to the shore of the gray, cold Atlantic. Secret Service agents, who are always assigned to protect the president, surrounded the compound. John Fitzgerald Kennedy was the president-elect. Shortly after noon, Richard Nixon sent his congratulations. Jack could now acknowledge his victory publicly.

Jack, Jackie, all the other Kennedys, and local campaign workers went to the Hyannis Port National Guard Armory to thank the voters and celebrate their victory. Jack read telegrams from President Eisenhower and Richard Nixon. He ended by saying, "So now my wife and I prepare for a new administration—and for a new baby."

The new baby didn't wait for the new administration. John Fitzgerald Kennedy Jr. was born on November 25, 1960—almost a month before he was expected. Because he was premature—not developed enough to live on his own—the baby had to be in an incubator for nine days. Jack visited the

The proud parents pose with John Fitzgerald Kennedy Jr. after his christening.

hospital several times a day to see his wife and baby son. When John Jr. and Jacqueline were strong enough to travel, the family flew to Florida to spend the Christmas holidays at the Kennedys' West Palm Beach home.

Other members of the Kennedy family were also there, and everyone admired the new baby. When Jack returned with his son, daughter, and wife to Georgetown, he and Jackie had only a short time to prepare for Inauguration Day. They would have to move from their Georgetown home to the White House.

While still in the hospital, Jackie had asked her secretary to bring her all the books she could find on the history and furnishings of the White House. She remembered that when she was 11 years old, her mother had taken her on a tour of the White House. At that time there had been no written material furnished to visitors and very little information available. Jackie was determined to remedy this situation.

On January 20, 1961, after a heavy snowfall the night before, Jackie, the Kennedys, the Fitzgeralds, the Bouviers, the Lees, the Auchinclosses, and a proud nation watched as John Fitzgerald Kennedy took the oath of office and became the 35th president of the United States. Snow-filled streets only added to the excitement of the gala day. Three hundred members of the National Guard had joined city workers to clear the parade route of snow, and a huge parade wound past the reviewing stand. Members of the armed forces paraded in their dress uniforms, flags waved, and bands from all over the country played as they marched past. A model of Jack's old PT 109, the boat from his navy days, even rolled by. Many of his old navy buddies were aboard, waving at him as the float passed. After a while, Jackie left the viewing stand to return to the White House. The new president, however, stayed to the very end.

Jack became the 35th president of the United States on January 20, 1961, when he took the oath of office.

When the new president and the First Lady entered the ballroom of the Mayflower Hotel to attend the first of many inaugural balls that evening, guests gasped in admiration. Jackie looked stunning in a slim white gown and a long white satin cape. When the couple arrived at the armory, their third stop, guests gave them a 20-minute standing ovation. Jackie left the festivities about midnight, but Jack attended two more balls.

Jackie looked elegant as she and Jack left the White House to attend several inaugural balls.

The day after the inauguration, the president plunged into business with a meeting of his cabinet and staff. Jackie had meetings with the White House staff; her press secretary, Tish Baldridge; and Caroline's nanny, Maude Shaw. She discussed plans to renovate—not redecorate—the White House, which the Kennedys found to be in terrible condition. Jackie wanted the rooms to have historical significance rather than just reflect the changing tastes of each First Lady. Her first priority, however, was getting the children's rooms in order.

The First Family enjoys a few moments of leisure, but notice that the telephone is still nearby.

Jackie converted the former solarium, or sunroom, on the third floor to a schoolroom. She arranged to have the children of some friends and some Kennedy cousins attend nursery school classes there with Caroline. Jackie wanted Caroline to have children her own age to learn and play with. When John Jr. was old enough, he would attend also.

In addition, Jackie had White House workers set aside part of the White House grounds for a playground. She had swings, a trampoline, a slide, a sandbox, and a tree house installed. There were places to keep pets—hamsters, rabbits, dogs, cats, and even a pet salamander belonging to one of Bobby Kennedy's children.

When Jackie Kennedy arrived in the White House, it was in a state of disrepair. The formal rooms were not coordinated, and the furniture had no historical relevance. She wanted to restore the White House to the grand house it should be, and she set up a committee to do so. She urged people to donate pieces of furniture or other objects that had once graced the White House. Objects of great historical and artistic value began to come in from all parts of the country. Everything from priceless paintings to a length of velvet for a pair of Lincoln chairs appeared. Jackie went down to the sub-basements of the White House. She found a beautiful desk, dust covered and scratched, which she had refinished for Jack's Oval Office. She also had marble busts of past presidents, oriental rugs, and various other pieces of furniture brought up and refurbished.

Jackie said, "Everything in the White House must have a reason for being there. It would be sacrilege merely to 'redecorate' it—a word I hate. It must be restored—and that has nothing to do with decoration. That is a question of scholarship." Her efforts resulted in a beautiful restoration. Jackie became the first person ever to take the American public on a televised tour of the White House. For this she received an Emmy Award in 1962 for public service.

Jackie poses in the state dining room while giving a tour of the White House for television viewers.

President Kennedy and his wife were noted for the elegance of their dinner parties. They shared a talent for making guests of all walks of life feel welcome and at ease. They both had great charm. Jackie's influence made Washington an elegant, intellectual place to be.

The First Lady (a title Jackie hated) had a stage built in the East Room and invited great artists from the fields of music, dance, drama, literature, and art to take part in dazzling evenings there. After dinner in the State Dining Room, guests would adjourn to the East Room. There, under sparkling crystal chandeliers, they would be treated to a program of music, ballet, or perhaps a new play.

At a glittering reception for Nobel Prize winners, the president chats with writer Pearl Buck while Jackie talks with poet Robert Frost.

George Balanchine arranged for famed dancers Margot Fonteyn and Rudolf Nureyev to perform at a state dinner. Cellist Pablo Casals, who was living in exile in Puerto Rico, agreed to play at the White House when the Kennedys personally invited him. Other guests included poet Carl Sandburg, composers Igor Stravinsky and Aaron Copland, violinist Isaac Stern, dramatist Tennessee Williams, and painter Andrew Wyeth. Sometimes new, unknown singers or jazz groups would perform, which helped them advance their careers.

Jackie's grace, style, and intelligence brought a new image of the White House and its occupants to people not only in the United States, but all over the world. Jackie was said to be the closest thing to a princess the American people had ever had. Young girls copied her hairdo, women admired her simple but elegant clothes. Beautiful, witty, and intelligent, she brought a new grace and sophistication to the nation's capital.

Jackie made a goodwill trip to India in March 1962. She met with Indira Gandhi, *second from left,* and Prime Minister Jawaharlal Nehru, *right.*

Young John and Caroline weren't the least bit awed by living in the White House. It was just the house where they lived and their daddy worked. Jackie worked hard to protect their privacy so they could be normal, natural children—in spite of their fame. Jackie carried on a war of independence with the press. The American public, however, loved catching glimpses of her and the children—John Jr. marching up and down the Truman balcony waving a small American flag or peeking out from under the president's desk. Newspapers and magazines printed photos of the children showing their father a dance they had learned and of Caroline with her pony, Macaroni.

Caroline rides her pony, Macaroni, on the White House grounds.

Jackie charmed President Charles de Gaulle on a state trip to France in May 1961. Here, they stand outside the Elysée Palace.

In early June 1961, Jackie accompanied President Kennedy to Europe, where he was to meet with Nikita Khrushchev of the Soviet Union in Austria. Before going to Austria, the Kennedys visited President Charles de Gaulle in France. Although the two presidents may have had some political disagreements, de Gaulle—and the Parisian public—were charmed by Jacqueline Kennedy. She addressed the people and conversed with President de Gaulle in perfect French. Crowds chanted *Zha-kee, Zha-kee.* She told President de Gaulle that she had read the French edition of his book and that her grandparents had been French. De Gaulle jokingly replied, "So were mine."

After leaving France, the president and First Lady went to Vienna, Austria. Again Jackie dazzled the crowds, foreign dignitaries, and the international press. From Vienna they flew to London for the christening of Anna Christina Radziwill, Lee's daughter. Lee had divorced her first husband and married Prince Stanislaus Radziwill, a Polish-born nobleman, in March 1959. President Kennedy then returned to Washington, but Jackie and Lee took a brief vacation in Greece.

On a state visit to Mexico, Jackie spoke to the people in Spanish, their native language.

In May 1962, Jackie christened the *Lafayette,* the nation's largest Polaris-firing submarine.

Jackie made many other state trips with her husband during his presidency and continued to fulfill her official duties as First Lady. She also became pregnant for the fifth time. On August 7, 1963, Jackie gave birth to a little boy. But Patrick Bouvier Kennedy was born with a breathing difficulty. The Kennedys prayed that he would live but knew that he might not. In spite of all the doctors' efforts, the baby died. Caroline and John, who had been promised a baby brother, were disappointed. Grief-stricken, Jackie and Jack buried the tiny child, their last.

Jackie and the president were given a warm welcome when they arrived in Dallas, Texas, on November 22, 1963. A little girl in the crowd gave Jackie the small bouquet of pink and yellow flowers.

5

Fateful Journey

To help Jackie recover from the death of her son, her sister Lee suggested that they take another trip together to the Mediterranean. Part of their vacation was spent on the yacht of Aristotle Onassis, a wealthy, Greek shipowner and business executive. He was a friend of Lee's, whom Jackie had met earlier. The sea air, the luxury of the yacht, the carefree days and nights, were just what Jackie needed.

When she returned to Washington, Jack was making plans to go to Texas. Racist and right-wing groups warned him not to go there, saying that his safety could not be guaranteed in their areas. But he was aware that a segment of the population in Texas disagreed with his stand on civil rights. Two factions of the Democratic Party in Texas were at odds, and he hoped his visit—with Vice President Lyndon Johnson, who was from Texas—would help heal the breach. He was also getting ready to begin his campaign for a second term as president. He *had* to win in Texas, which at that time was the largest state in the union. However, if the Democrats were fighting amongst themselves, the Republican candidate might win the election there.

Jackie decided to go with her husband. They arrived in San Antonio, Texas, on November 21. A sea of smiling, waving, cheering people, many of Spanish descent, greeted them. Jackie won their admiration by speaking to them in Spanish.

From San Antonio, they flew to Houston and then to Fort Worth, where they spent the night. The next morning, they attended a breakfast given for them by the Fort Worth Chamber of Commerce. When Jackie appeared at the breakfast, a little late, she charmed the audience with her strawberry pink suit and matching pillbox hat. The president looked at her admiringly and said, "Why is it no one cares what Lyndon and I wear?" The mood was upbeat.

From Fort Worth they flew to Love Field in Dallas. A crowd of enthusiastic people greeted the presidential party and tried to reach through the wire fence to touch the president and First Lady.

A little girl, helped by her mother, offered Jackie a bouquet of flowers. Jackie, who already carried a bouquet of red roses, took the rather wilted flowers and smilingly thanked the little girl. A crowd estimated at 250,000 lined the route of the presidential motorcade. The crowds were waving and cheering. Jackie and the president sat in the back of an open car, with Governor and Mrs. Connally seated on "jump" seats in front of them. A Secret Service man drove the car, and another sat next to him with a rifle on a rack in front of him.

The presidential motorcade passes through Dallas, moments before the assassination occurred.

Several cars full of Secret Service men followed the president's car. Mrs. Connally turned and spoke over her shoulder to the Kennedys. "You can't say Dallas wasn't friendly," she smiled.

Her words were drowned out by a sharp crack that sounded like a car backfiring. Jackie turned to face Jack. The president was starting to fall forward, his hand at his throat. Governor Connally cried out, then slumped forward. Then came another loud blast, and the back of the president's head was torn away by a bullet.

Jackie, in a haze of terror for Jack, saw that Clint Hill, a Secret Service agent from the car behind, was running along the road and trying to climb into

Jack slumped into Jackie's arms after an assassin's bullet hit him in the head. The car sped away to the hospital.

the president's car. Jackie crawled over the back-seat and reached out to help him. He grasped her hand, pulled himself into the car, pushed Jackie down to protect her, and threw himself over the president's body.

The driver radioed the nearest hospital and sped to its doors. Doctors and orderlies met the president's car and rushed him into Trauma Room I. Governor Connally was taken to another emergency room. Everything possible was done to bring back a spark of life to the president, but the situation was hopeless.

For the second time, John Kennedy received the last rites of the Catholic church. Jackie stood by and joined in the prayers led by two priests from nearby Holy Trinity Church. President John F. Kennedy was dead, and the world would never be the same again.

Vice President Johnson, not knowing if the shooting was part of a conspiracy, wanted to get back to Washington as soon as possible. Jackie (still in her blood-stained pink suit), Lyndon Johnson, Mrs. Johnson, and other members of the presidential party drove from the hospital to board *Air Force One*. Also on board was the body of the nation's fallen president. Jackie stood next to the vice president, with Mrs. Johnson on his other side, as Judge Sarah Hughes administered the oath of office.

Vice President Lyndon B. Johnson is sworn in as president aboard the presidential plane. Jackie stands at his side.

When the party landed in Washington, Jackie followed her husband's casket off the plane. Bobby Kennedy was there to meet her. He helped her with the details of his brother's funeral. Putting her own anguish aside, Jackie began planning her husband's funeral. She wanted Jack's funeral to be just like Lincoln's, since both presidents had been assassinated. Planning the funeral also helped her direct her thoughts away from the awful moments in Dallas.

In her blood-splattered clothing, Jackie watches as Jack's dead body is placed in an ambulance at Andrews Air Force Base, near Washington, D.C.

The day after its return from Dallas, President Kennedy's body lay in its flag-draped casket on the same bier (or stand) that held the body of Abraham Lincoln in the Rotunda of the Capitol. All day and far into the night, long lines of mourners stood in the biting cold outside the Capitol, waiting their turn to bid their president a sorrowful good-bye. After the last mourner had passed the casket, Jackie and Caroline slipped into the Rotunda. As they knelt before the casket, Jackie kissed the flag that draped it. Caroline slipped her small hand beneath the flag, as if to get as close as possible to the father she would never see again.

Jackie and Caroline knelt beside Jack's casket as it lay in the Capitol Rotunda. Caroline slipped her hand under the flag.

The next day, most of the world watched as the grieving widow and her two small children emerged from St. Matthew's Cathedral, where the requiem mass for the president had been held. As the funeral procession formed in the street, a riderless black horse, its stirrups hanging backward from the saddle, trotted beside the caisson, the two-wheeled cart that carried the casket. Eight matched gray horses pulled the caisson. As the family stood watching, Jackie stooped down and whispered something to her son. John raised his tiny hand and gravely saluted his dead father.

Jackie, *back center,* walks behind the caisson. Dignitaries from around the world follow in the mournful procession.

Jackie waits, with Caroline and John Jr., for Jack's body to be put on the caisson for the start of the procession to the Capitol.

Then the mourners began a sad march to Arlington National Cemetery. Among them were dignitaries from around the world, family members, friends, and government officials. Jackie, her head covered by a black veil but held high, marched with them. At the cemetery, she lit an eternal flame over her husband's grave, listened to the solemn prayers being recited, and received the flag from her husband's casket. When she returned to the White House, she graciously greeted the international dignitaries who had attended the funeral. Jackie was able to rise above her grief, and her courage earned her the respect and admiration of the world.

Later that evening, family members and a few friends joined her. They were marking yet another occasion with Jackie, Caroline, and John. It was November 25, John's third birthday.

On his third birthday, John salutes his dead father.

In January 1966, Caroline, Jackie, and John left New York for a skiing holiday in Switzerland.

6

Aftermath

After Jackie and the children left the White House, they moved back to the Georgetown area of Washington for a short time. But Jackie became very depressed. Everything around her reminded her of Jack. Tourists and members of the press jammed the street she lived on, hoping to catch a glimpse of her and the children. Jackie worried about how to bring up the children so they would have a normal life.

Eventually Jackie decided to move to New York, where she and the children would not be the focus of so much attention. She bought a 15-room apartment on Fifth Avenue across from Central Park, where she had played as a child. Caroline attended the Convent of the Sacred Heart, and when he was old enough, John enrolled in St. David's School.

Robert F. Kennedy, one of Jack's younger brothers, was assassinated in 1968 while campaigning for the Democratic presidential nomination.

Sometimes, when Jackie walked the children home from school, they strolled down the street like any ordinary family, licking ice cream cones with great enjoyment.

In March 1968, Senator Robert Kennedy (Jack's brother Bobby) announced that he was going to run for the Democratic presidential nomination, although Jackie had tried to convince him not to. In June 1968, the country was once more torn apart by tragedy. As he was leaving the Ambassador Hotel in Los Angeles on the night of the California primary election, a shot rang out. Bobby dropped to the floor, mortally wounded. A young Palestinian Arab, Sirhan Sirhan, admitted to the killing.

Jackie attended Bobby's funeral with John and Caroline, now five years older than they had been when their father had been assassinated. Jackie was convinced that this latest senseless violence was a conspiracy, and that her children would be the next victims. She turned to a man who had been a friend, a man who could offer security for her family—Aristotle Onassis.

Jackie married Aristotle Onassis on October 20, 1968. The wedding took place in Greece.

Ari spent part of the summer at Hyannis Port, getting to know the family—especially Caroline and John. His own children, 18-year-old Christina and 20-year-old Alexander, were rather hostile toward Jackie. But Ari proposed marriage, and Jackie accepted. On October 20, 1968, she and Ari were married on Scorpios, a Greek Island owned by Onassis. Shortly after their marriage, Ari went on a business trip, leaving Jackie on Scorpios with Caroline and John. Reluctantly, Jackie sent the children back to school in New York with her mother and stepfather.

It wasn't long before the marriage was on shaky ground. Jackie's marriage was greatly criticized in the United States. Ari was almost twice her age, and he was a "foreigner," people said. She was accused of marrying him for his money. Christina Onassis resented her new stepmother, and let her know it. Then in January 1973, Alexander Onassis, Ari's beloved son, was killed in an airplane accident just after his 24th birthday. Ari seemed to age overnight. He became bitter and depressed. And he began to blame Jackie, saying she had brought him bad luck.

Jackie began splitting her time between Greece and the United States. When Ari came to New York, he stayed at Jackie's apartment on Fifth Avenue, but he and Jackie were growing further and further apart. Jackie had obtained a business office a few blocks from her home, where she worked on organizing the John F. Kennedy Memorial Library. She was also the moving force behind the building of the Kennedy Center for the Performing Arts in Washington, D.C. She joined the Municipal Arts Society in New York and led the fight to save Grand Central Station from the wrecker's ball and restore it to its former grandeur.

Jackie prepares to turn the switch that will light Grand Central Station, one of New York's architectural landmarks.

Jackie, *right,* with Ari's daughter, Christina Onassis

Jackie needed these outlets for her organizing abilities, which she had also demonstrated in the White House. She also had a strong desire to preserve the things in American culture that are beautiful and artistic. Ari didn't share these interests, and the marriage continued to disintegrate. And although Ari didn't realize it, he had become a very sick man. In December 1973, Ari entered Lenox Hill Hospital and was diagnosed as having myasthenia gravis. Doctors knew very little about this debilitating disease of the muscles. In 1975 Ari died in Greece, while Jackie was in New York. She and the children returned to Greece for the funeral. Jackie and Christina became involved in a bitter 18-month legal battle over the Onassis estate. They finally agreed to a settlement of $26 million for Jackie, $6 million of which went for taxes. Jackie returned to New York a very rich woman.

After the death of Aristotle Onassis, Jackie felt she had to establish a new identity for herself and achieve success based on her own merits. She was not as socially active as she had been. She spent more evenings at home, helping John with his homework, reading, painting, sketching, or watching television. Then, once again, she did the unexpected.

She went to work in the editorial department of Viking Press. She had always loved languages and literature, and she turned out to be a good editor. She enjoyed working on manuscripts and had a flair for it.

After two years with Viking, Jackie moved to Doubleday, a larger company. She was highly regarded there also. She was friendly, cooperative, and had a keen eye for what was good and bad in literature. She worked three days a week, Tuesday through Thursday, in a small, book-crammed office. The books she edited reflected her eclectic tastes and wide variety of interests.

Jackie fiercely protected the privacy of her children, but not with restrictions and prohibitions. As the Kennedy children grew, travel and sports became part of their education. Jackie taught

Caroline and Jackie at a New Jersey horse show

Caroline and John to ride horseback, and she took them sledding, skiing, swimming, and boating. They kept in touch with their Kennedy cousins and spent part of their summers at Hyannis Port. Later Jackie built a summer home on Martha's Vineyard.

As Caroline and John were growing up, Jackie supported their interests. She encouraged John to take part in Outward Bound (a program that teaches survival skills) and supported his desire to attend Brown University rather than Harvard, his father's school. After graduating from Brown in 1983, John attended a work-study program in India. He earned his law degree from New York University in 1989. Caroline took a year to study art through a program in London sponsored by Sotheby's, the prestigious art auctioneers. Afterward she attended Radcliffe College and graduated in 1980. She then earned her law degree from Harvard University. Both Caroline and John became centered and well-adjusted adults, who always had their mother's affection.

Jackie had many escorts after she became a widow for the second time. Gradually she chose one favorite companion, Maurice Tempelsman. A diamond merchant with international connections, Maurice shared all Jackie's interests. He was a lover of the arts in many forms: painting, sculpture, architecture, music, the theater. He dressed well and loved to read and travel. With him Jackie found the equilibrium and peace of mind she had sought.

Jackie, *left,* fought to preserve Grand Central Station, the low building seen in the background.

Maurice was devoted to Jackie's children, as they were to him. They shared simple pleasures—walks in Central Park and picnics with Jackie's three grandchildren, Tatiana, Rose, and John (the children of Caroline and her husband, Ed Schlossberg, an artist and designer). Her grandchildren afforded Jackie some of the happiest times of her later years.

In 1984 Jackie testified before a New York legislative committee about a bill relating to the preservation of historic churches.

Jackie's life seemed pleasant and fulfilling until February 1994, when she announced that she had cancer. Her doctors had diagnosed it as non-Hodgkin's lymphoma, which affects the lymphocytes, or white blood cells. Maurice told Jackie they would fight the cancer together. Jackie underwent chemotherapy treatments, in which doctors administer a variety of strong drugs to destroy the cancer cells. Although chemotherapy is often effective in treating certain types of cancer, it also has many undesirable side effects such as nausea and an increased risk of infection. Jackie courageously said the treatments weren't so bad—she could read a book while they were administered. She continued working at Doubleday until just a few weeks before her death, when she finally had to quit.

When she went back to the hospital for a checkup, she was told the cancer had spread to other organs. There was nothing more the doctors could do for her. Knowing she would die, Jackie could have chosen the best hospital care available. Instead, she dismissed herself from the hospital and went home. She chose to die as she had lived, in privacy, with courage and dignity.

On May 19, Jackie's parish priest, Monsignor Georges Bardes of Manhattan's Church of St. Thomas More, came to visit her and give her the last rites of the Catholic church. Caroline, John, and Maurice Tempelsman were at her bedside, as she had wished, when she died that night.

The church of St. Ignatius Loyola, where Jackie had been baptized and confirmed, was filled to capacity on May 23, the morning of her funeral mass. John and Caroline had planned the ceremony and prayers, with the help of the clergy.

John and Caroline follow their mother's casket out of St. Ignatius Loyola Church in New York City.

Senator Ted Kennedy, Jack's youngest brother, gave the eulogy. He said, "The former First Lady was a blessing to us and to the nation, and a lesson to the world on how to do things right—how to be a mother, how to appreciate history, how to be courageous. She graced our history, she graced our lives."

As Jackie wished, she was to be buried in Arlington National Cemetery, next to her first husband, Jack Kennedy. After the mass in New York City, most of the mourners took planes to Washington to attend the burial services there. President Bill Clinton met them at the airport and joined the procession to the cemetery. The service was private and solemn. The Navy Sea Chanters sang the same hymn they had sung for President Kennedy. President Clinton said, "God gave her very great gifts and imposed upon her great burdens. She bore them all with dignity and grace and uncommon common sense." As the president spoke, the eternal flame that Jackie herself had lit three decades earlier, flickered in the May sunshine. She was buried between her husband Jack and her stillborn daughter. Her son Patrick lies on the other side of Jack.

Caroline and John knelt and kissed their mother's casket. John paused at his father's grave and touched it, and he stopped again at Bobby's grave.

Finally, all the mourners left, and Jackie was alone with Jack and her two dead children. Before she died, she had whispered, "I'll soon be with you, my little angels."

A lifetime had passed since an exotic beauty had floated down the stairs at a debutante ball. She had indeed found a priceless pearl—purchased with courage, dignity, and grace.

Jacqueline Bouvier Kennedy Onassis (1929–1994)

Epilogue

President Bill Clinton said that Jackie Kennedy Onassis "was a model of courage and dignity for all Americans and the entire world." He said later, "She was an astonishing woman. She captivated the world with her intelligence, elegance, and grace, more than any woman of our time. Even in the face of impossible tragedy, she carried the grief of her family and the nation with a calm power that somehow reassured all the rest of us."

Senator Ted Kennedy said, "Jackie would have preferred to be just herself, but the world insisted that she be a legend, too. She never wanted public notice—in part, I think, because it brought back painful memories of an unbearable sorrow, endured in the glare of a million lights."

Lady Bird Johnson, who became First Lady when Vice President Johnson became president, said: "In times of hope she captured our hearts. In tragedy, her courage helped to salve a nation's grief. She was an image of beauty and romance and leaves an empty place in the world as we have known it....I always thought of her as my friend. I feel a poignant sense of loss, and a larger one for the nation."

Arthur Schlesinger, special assistant to President Kennedy and author of *A Thousand Days: John F. Kennedy in the White House*, said: "She was a woman of fierce independence....One recalls above all the quiet but implacable determination, amid the uncontrollable blazes of publicity, to live her own life."